How to Build a Successful Personal Brand

A Step-by-Step Guide to Becoming an Authority in Your Field and Achieving Your Career Goals

The Fix-It Guy

Copyright © The Fix-It Guy

Table of Contents

Introduction

Hey there, fellow go-getters and aspiring trailblazers! Have you ever dreamed of making your mark in the world, of being that shining star in your field, but found yourself lost in the daunting maze of personal branding? Well, guess what? You're not alone, and I've been there too!

Picture this: You're at a networking event, trying to introduce yourself, but the words stumble out, and you end up sounding like a broken record. Or maybe you're scrolling through social media, marveling at how some people effortlessly exude confidence and authority while you're stuck wondering, "How on earth do they do that?"

Fear not, because help has arrived! Welcome to "How to Build a Successful Personal Brand: A Step-by-Step Guide to Becoming an Authority in Your Field and Achieving Your Career Goals." This isn't just another self-help book; it's your ticket to personal branding nirvana, your secret weapon to conquering the professional world with style, substance, and a splash of pizzazz!

Imagine a life where you're not just recognized, but celebrated for your expertise. Envision a future where your name evokes trust and admiration, where opportunities knock on your door, eager to be a part of your journey. Sounds exciting, right? Well, this book is your backstage pass to that exhilarating reality!

But hold on, it's not all serious business here! Along the way, we'll share stories that will make you chuckle, anecdotes that will tug at your heartstrings, and advice that's as practical as your favorite pair of jeans. Personal branding isn't about putting on a show; it's about embracing your unique quirks, talents, and passions, and showcasing them to the world in a way that leaves an indelible mark.

So, dear reader, if you're ready to transform your career, step into the spotlight with confidence, and build a personal brand that's as authentic as it is compelling, then buckle up and dive right in! Together, we'll embark on a thrilling adventure, unlocking the secrets of personal branding, one chapter at a time.

Get ready to redefine your success story because, trust me, the world is waiting to know your name, your brand, and your extraordinary journey. Let's do this!

Chapter 1

Defining Your Personal Brand

Identifying Your Unique Value Proposition

In the vast and bustling marketplace of ideas and talents, it's easy to get lost in the crowd. But fear not! This chapter is your guiding star, illuminating the path toward defining your brand. Your journey begins by uncovering the essence of who you are and what makes you exceptional.

Your unique value proposition (UVP) is the magic potion that sets you apart from the rest. It's that special blend of skills, experiences, and qualities that make you, well, you. Think of it as your personal brand's DNA, the core elements that define your identity in the professional world.

Why Is It Important?
1. Stand Out in the Crowd: In a sea of professionals, your UVP is your life raft. It helps you rise above the

noise and capture the attention of your audience. When people can see what makes you unique, they're more likely to remember you.

2. Attract the Right Opportunities: Whether you're aiming for a dream job or seeking clients for your business, your UVP acts as a magnet. It draws in opportunities that align with your strengths and passions. Imagine finding opportunities that resonate with your core skills and values – that's the power of a well-defined UVP.

3. Build Credibility: A strong UVP builds trust. When you can articulate what sets you apart, it signals confidence and expertise. Others perceive you as someone who knows their stuff and can deliver exceptional results.

How to Identify Your Unique Value Proposition

1. Self-Reflection: Start by reflecting on your skills, passions, and experiences. What are you exceptionally good at? What do you love doing? What unique experiences have shaped you? Your UVP often lies at the intersection of your skills and passions.

2. Feedback: Seek feedback from colleagues, mentors, and friends. They can offer valuable insights into your strengths and qualities that you might not see in yourself. Sometimes, an outside perspective can provide a fresh angle on your unique qualities.

3. Market Research: Look at others in your field or industry. What do they offer, and how can you differentiate yourself? Identify gaps or areas where you can excel. Your UVP should address a specific need or solve a particular problem in your industry.

4. Test and Refine: Don't be afraid to experiment and test different aspects of your UVP. As you gain more experience and feedback, refine your proposition to make it even more compelling.

Remember, your unique value proposition isn't set in stone. It can evolve as you grow personally and professionally. Embrace the process of self-discovery, and don't shy away from showcasing what makes you extraordinary. With a clear and compelling UVP, you'll be well on your way to building a personal brand that leaves a lasting impression.

Assessing Your Strengths and Weaknesses

Understanding your strengths and weaknesses is like having a detailed map of your skills and areas for improvement. It's a crucial step in the personal branding journey, as it helps you play to your strengths and work on your weaknesses strategically.

Why Assessing Your Strengths and Weaknesses Matters:

1. Maximize Your Strengths: By identifying your strengths, you can focus your energy on what you do best. Whether it's excellent communication skills, creativity, or analytical prowess, leveraging your strengths amplifies your impact and enhances your brand.

2. Address Your Weaknesses: No one is perfect, and that's okay. Acknowledging your weaknesses isn't a sign of failure; it's a step toward growth. When you recognize your weak points, you can take proactive measures to improve or compensate for them. This awareness is invaluable in personal and professional development.

3. Strategic Decision-Making: Understanding your strengths and weaknesses empowers you to make strategic decisions. You can choose opportunities that align with your strengths and avoid situations that heavily rely on your weaknesses. This strategic approach ensures you're always in a position to excel.

How to Assess Your Strengths and Weaknesses:

1. Self-Reflection: Take some time for introspection. What skills do you excel at? In what areas do you struggle? Be honest with yourself. Consider feedback from past experiences and recognize patterns in your successes and challenges.

2. Feedback from Others: Seek input from colleagues, friends, and mentors. They might offer insights that you haven't considered. Others often see strengths in us that we underestimate and weaknesses that we overlook.

3. Professional Assessments: Consider using professional assessments and tools designed to evaluate strengths and weaknesses. These assessments can provide structured insights and help you understand your personality traits, work styles, and areas of improvement.

Clarifying Your Brand's Purpose and Mission

Your brand's purpose and mission are the heart and soul of your brand. They define why you do what you do and what you aim to achieve. Clarity in your purpose and mission not only guides your actions but also resonates with your audience on a deeper level.

Why Clarifying Your Brand's Purpose and Mission Matters:

1. Inspires and Motivates: A clear purpose inspires you to wake up every morning with enthusiasm and determination. It fuels your passion and keeps you focused on your goals, even in challenging times.

2. Connects Emotionally: People connect with brands that have a purpose beyond profit. When your mission resonates with your audience's values and aspirations, it creates an emotional connection. This connection fosters loyalty and trust.

3. Guides Decision-Making: Your purpose and mission act as a compass, guiding your decisions and actions. They help you prioritize opportunities and initiatives that align with your core beliefs. This alignment ensures authenticity and consistency in your brand.

How to Clarify Your Brand's Purpose and Mission:

1. Identify Your Values: What do you stand for? Identify your core values, the principles that are non-negotiable for you. Your purpose should align with these values, reflecting what truly matters to you.

2. Define Your Impact: Consider the impact you want to make in your field or community. How do you want to change lives or contribute to the betterment of society? Your mission should articulate the change you aspire to create.

3. Craft a Clear Statement: Distill your purpose and mission into a concise, compelling statement. It should be clear, inspirational, and easy to understand. Your purpose statement outlines the reason for your existence, while your mission statement defines your specific objectives and actions to fulfill that purpose.

Remember, your strengths and weaknesses are the building blocks of your brand, and your purpose and mission are the guiding lights. With a deep understanding of these elements, you're well-equipped to craft a personal brand that not only stands out but also resonates with authenticity and purpose.

Chapter 2

Understanding Your Target Audience

Creating Buyer Personas

In the ever-changing landscape of personal branding, one truth remains constant: understanding your audience is the key to success. This chapter delves deep into the art and science of understanding your target audience, helping you create connections that go beyond superficial interactions and transform casual followers into loyal advocates.

Why Understanding Your Target Audience Matters:

1. Tailored Communication: Your audience comprises diverse individuals with unique needs and preferences. Understanding them allows you to tailor your communication style, ensuring that your message resonates with specific segments of your audience. One size doesn't fit all, and personalized communication is the secret sauce to building lasting relationships.

2. Anticipating Needs: By comprehending your audience's challenges, desires, and pain points, you can anticipate their needs. This foresight enables you to offer solutions before they even voice their concerns, positioning you as a reliable and empathetic authority in your field.

3. Building Trust: When your audience feels understood, they trust you. Trust is the cornerstone of any meaningful relationship, and it's no different in the realm of personal branding. Trust fosters loyalty, encouraging your audience to engage with your content, products, or services confidently.

Creating Buyer Personas
Buyer personas are detailed, semi-fictional representations of your ideal customers or clients. They embody the characteristics, goals, challenges, and behaviors of your target audience segments. Creating accurate buyer personas is akin to having a backstage pass to your audience's thoughts and emotions.

How to Create Buyer Personas:

1. Research: Conduct in-depth research to gather insights about your audience. Utilize surveys, interviews, social media analytics, and website data to understand their demographics, preferences, behaviors, and pain points. The more you know, the more accurate your buyer personas will be.

2. Identify Patterns: Analyze the gathered data to identify common patterns and trends among your audience segments. Look for similarities in age, location, interests, challenges, and goals. These patterns form the basis of your buyer personas.

3. Persona Creation: Create distinct buyer personas based on the identified patterns. Give each persona a name, background story, job title, interests, goals, challenges, and preferred communication channels. The more detailed and human-like your personas are, the easier it becomes to empathize with them and tailor your strategies accordingly.

4. Utilize Personas Strategically: Once your personas are created, integrate them into your content creation, marketing, and communication strategies. Craft content that directly addresses the needs and aspirations of each persona. Whether you're writing blog posts, creating social media campaigns, or designing products, ensure that your strategies align with the personas' characteristics.

Understanding your audience and creating detailed buyer personas is the secret recipe for personal branding success. It empowers you to engage authentically, anticipate needs, and build meaningful connections. So, grab your magnifying glass, dive into the depths of your audience's psyche, and get ready to create a personal brand that speaks directly to the hearts and minds of your ideal followers.

Knowing Your Ideal Clients or Employers

In the world of personal branding, precision is your superpower. Knowing your ideal clients or employers is akin to having a laser-focused radar that ensures you attract the right opportunities and build meaningful relationships. This chapter is your compass for navigating the intricate landscapes of personal and professional connections.

Why Knowing Your Ideal Clients or Employers Matters:

1. Efficient Targeting: Understanding the specific characteristics of your ideal clients or employers allows you to allocate your time and resources efficiently. Rather than casting a wide net, you can direct your efforts where they are most likely to yield results.

2. Alignment of Values: Personal satisfaction and success come from working with individuals or organizations that align with your values and goals. By knowing your ideal clients or employers, you can ensure that your partnerships are built on shared principles, making collaboration more enjoyable and meaningful.

3. Tailored Messaging: Your communication becomes far more persuasive when it's tailored to the needs and expectations of your ideal clients or employers. You can address their pain points, desires, and objectives, making it more likely that they'll resonate with your message and offerings.

Identifying Your Niche

Your niche is your corner of the world, the territory you claim as your own. It's the area of expertise or the specific market segment where you excel and offer unique value. Finding and defining your niche is a critical step in personal branding that helps you stand out in a crowded marketplace.

How to Identify Your Niche:

1. **Self-Assessment:** Start by assessing your skills, experiences, and passions. What do you excel at? What topics or areas genuinely interest and excite you? Your niche should align with your strengths and passions to keep you motivated and engaged.

2. **Market Research:** Study your field or industry. What are the current trends, challenges, and gaps in the market? Is there an underserved segment that you could cater to? Identifying opportunities within your field can lead you to your niche.

3. **Competitor Analysis:** Analyze your competitors. What areas do they dominate, and where might there be an opening for you to carve out your niche? Competitors can provide valuable insights into market dynamics and potential niches.

4. Audience Feedback: Listen to your audience. What topics or offerings generate the most engagement and interest from them? Your audience's preferences can help guide you toward a niche that resonates.

5. Test and Refine: As you explore potential niches, be prepared to test and refine your focus. It's okay to adapt and pivot based on your experiences and the feedback you receive from your audience.

Knowing your ideal clients or employers and identifying your niche sharpens your personal brand's focus and makes you the go-to expert in your chosen domain. It's not about limiting yourself but about standing out and excelling in the areas that matter most to you and your audience. So, embrace the process of defining your unique space, and get ready to flourish in your personal branding journey.

Chapter 3

Crafting Your Brand Identity

Choosing the Right Name and Logo

Your brand identity is like the face of your brand – it's what people recognize and remember you by. In this chapter, we'll dive into the art of crafting a brand identity that not only represents who you are but also leaves a lasting impression on your audience. From choosing the right name to designing a logo that speaks volumes, get ready to infuse your brand with personality and authenticity.

Your brand's name and logo are the cornerstones of your identity. They are the first things people notice, and they should encapsulate the essence of your brand in a nutshell.

Choosing the Right Name:

1. Reflect Your Identity: Your brand's name should reflect your personality, values, and the core message you want to convey. It could be your name or a creative representation of your expertise and uniqueness.

2. Memorability is Key: A memorable name sticks in people's minds. Aim for simplicity and clarity – a name that people can easily recall and share with others. Avoid overly complicated or lengthy names that might be hard to remember.

3. Check Availability: Ensure that the name you choose is available as a domain name for your website and across social media platforms. Consistency in your online presence is vital for brand recognition.

Designing Your Logo:

1. Simplicity Speaks Volumes: A simple and clean logo is often the most effective. Think of iconic logos like Apple or Nike, they are uncomplicated yet instantly recognizable. Avoid clutter and aim for a design that is easy to reproduce across various mediums.

2. Relevance and Symbolism: Your logo should be relevant to your field and personal brand. Consider incorporating symbols or elements related to your expertise. Symbolism can create a powerful connection with your audience.

3. Color Psychology: Colors evoke emotions and convey meanings. Choose colors that align with your brand's personality. For example, blue signifies trust and professionalism, while green represents growth and harmony. Understand the psychological impact of colors on your audience.

4. Professional Design: If design isn't your forte, consider investing in a professional graphic designer. A well-designed logo is a worthwhile investment that pays off in creating a polished and credible brand image.

Remember, your brand's name and logo are your visual ambassadors. They should resonate with your audience, leaving a positive and memorable impression. Take your time in choosing and designing these elements, ensuring they align harmoniously with your personal brand's identity. With the right name and logo, you're not just creating an identity, you're crafting a brand legacy that will stand the test of time.

Designing Your Visual Identity

Your visual identity is the artistic expression of your brand. It's the visual language that communicates your essence to the world. In this section, we'll explore the vital components of crafting a visually appealing and cohesive brand identity.

1. Consistent Aesthetics: Choose a consistent color palette, typography, and imagery style that reflects your brand personality. Consistency across all visual elements, from your website to social media posts, creates a cohesive and professional look.

2. Imagery and Photography: Select images and photographs that align with your brand message. Whether it's professional photoshoots or curated stock images, ensure they convey the emotions and values you want to associate with your brand.

3. Logo Usage: Establish guidelines for logo usage, including size, placement, and clear space. Consistent logo application maintains brand recognition and reinforces your visual identity.

4. Website and Social Media Design: Your website and social media profiles are often the first touchpoints for your audience. Design them in a user-friendly manner, ensuring easy navigation and a visually appealing layout. Use your chosen color scheme and typography consistently across these platforms.

5. Branded Materials: Extend your visual identity to business cards, letterheads, presentations, and other promotional materials. A cohesive design across all materials reinforces your brand image and professionalism.

Defining Your Brand's Voice and Tone

Your brand's voice and tone are the auditory elements of your brand. They dictate how you communicate with your audience, the words you use, the emotions you convey, and the personality you exude.

Defining Your Brand's Voice:

1. Personality Traits: Determine the personality traits that define your brand, are you witty, formal, friendly, or authoritative? Your voice should reflect these traits consistently.

2. Language Style: Choose a language style that resonates with your audience. It could be casual and conversational or formal and professional, depending on your target demographic and industry.

3. Consistency: Maintain consistency in your voice across all communication channels. Whether you're writing blog posts, social media updates, or email newsletters, your voice should remain recognizable and true to your brand.

Defining Your Brand's Tone:

1. Adaptability: While your voice remains consistent, your tone can adapt based on the context. It could be empathetic and comforting in a customer support interaction or inspirational and motivational in a blog post.

2. Understanding Your Audience: Tailor your tone based on your audience's preferences and emotions. Understand their needs, concerns, and aspirations, and adjust your tone to resonate with their feelings.

3. Emotional Connection: Use your tone to create an emotional connection with your audience. A genuine and empathetic tone fosters trust and encourages meaningful engagement.

By carefully designing your visual identity and defining your brand's voice and tone, you create a multi-sensory experience for your audience. Consistency and authenticity in these elements reinforce your brand message, making it more memorable and relatable. Remember, your visual and auditory cues are powerful tools, use them wisely to leave a lasting impact on your audience.

Consistency and authenticity in these elements reinforce your brand message, making it more memorable and relatable.

Chapter 4

Online Presence and Reputation Management

Building a Strong Online Presence

In the digital age, your online presence is often the first impression you make. This chapter is your guide to creating a powerful and positive online footprint. From establishing your presence on various platforms to managing your reputation effectively, we'll explore the strategies that will elevate your personal brand in the virtual realm.

1. Professional Website: Your website is your online home. Ensure it's well-designed, user-friendly, and showcases your expertise, portfolio, and achievements. Regularly update it with fresh content to demonstrate your ongoing involvement and expertise in your field.

2. Social Media Mastery: Choose social media platforms that align with your brand and target audience. Whether it's LinkedIn for professional networking, Instagram for visual storytelling, or Twitter for real-time updates, maintain active and engaging profiles.

Consistent posting and interaction with your audience are key.

3. Content Creation: Content is king in the digital world. Create valuable and relevant content such as blog posts, videos, podcasts, or infographics that showcase your expertise. Share your knowledge generously and position yourself as an authority in your field.

4. Search Engine Optimization (SEO): Optimize your online content for search engines to ensure it ranks higher in search results. Use relevant keywords, create quality backlinks, and improve your website's loading speed to enhance your visibility to potential audiences.

5. Professional Networking: Engage in online professional networks and communities related to your field. Participate in discussions, share insights, and connect with influencers and peers. Networking not only expands your reach but also enhances your credibility.

6. Online Portfolios: If applicable, create an online portfolio showcasing your work, projects, or achievements. Visual representations of your skills and accomplishments provide tangible proof of your expertise.

7. Consistent Branding: Maintain a consistent brand image across all online platforms. Use the same profile picture, bio, and messaging to ensure recognition. Consistency fosters trust and reinforces your brand identity.

Remember, building a strong online presence is not just about visibility; it's about creating a genuine connection with your audience. Engage authentically, provide value, and be responsive to your audience's needs. Your online presence should reflect your personality, expertise, and passion, establishing you as a go-to resource in your field. Stay authentic, stay engaged, and watch your online presence flourish.

Leveraging Social Media for Personal Branding

Social media is not just a platform for sharing cat videos and vacation photos; it's a powerful tool for personal branding when used strategically. Here's how you can leverage social media to amplify your brand:

1. Choose the Right Platforms: Identify the social media platforms where your target audience is most active. LinkedIn is excellent for professional networking, Twitter for real-time updates and thought leadership, Instagram for visual storytelling, and YouTube for video content. Tailor your content to fit the platform's strengths.

2. Content is Key: Create and curate content that showcases your expertise and interests. Share industry-related articles, your insights, behind-the-scenes glimpses, and success stories. Consistency is vital; establish a posting schedule to keep your audience engaged.

3. Engage Authentically: Don't just broadcast; engage with your audience. Respond to comments, participate in discussions, and acknowledge your followers. Authentic interactions foster a sense of community and trust.

4. Visual Appeal: Invest in visually appealing content. Use high-quality images, graphics, and videos to capture attention. Aesthetically pleasing content reflects professionalism and attention to detail.

5. Personal Touch: Let your personality shine through. Share personal anecdotes, hobbies, and interests. People connect with real, relatable individuals, so don't be afraid to show the human side of your brand.

6. Collaborate and Network: Collaborate with influencers and thought leaders in your field. Guest blogging, joint social media campaigns, or collaborations on podcasts or videos can expand your reach and credibility.

Managing Your Online Reputation

Your online reputation is your digital currency. Here's how to safeguard and enhance it:

1. Google Yourself: Regularly search your name to see what others find when they look you up. Address any inconsistencies, outdated information, or negative content promptly.

2. Privacy Settings: Understand the privacy settings on your social media accounts. Control who can see your posts, photos, and personal information. Regularly review and update these settings.

3. Online Etiquette: Practice good online etiquette. Be respectful and professional in your interactions. Avoid engaging in online arguments or sharing controversial opinions that might damage your reputation.

4. Online Reviews: If applicable, encourage satisfied clients or colleagues to leave positive reviews on platforms like Google, LinkedIn, or industry-specific websites. Address negative reviews diplomatically and professionally.

5. Monitoring Tools: Use online reputation monitoring tools to keep track of mentions of your name or brand.

These tools can alert you to any new content or discussions related to you, allowing you to respond promptly.

6. Apologize and Learn: If you make a mistake online, acknowledge it, apologize if necessary, and learn from the experience. Transparency and accountability can enhance your reputation in the long run.

Remember, your online presence and reputation are valuable assets. By leveraging social media strategically and managing your online presence proactively, you can shape a positive and influential personal brand that opens doors to opportunities and meaningful connections. Stay mindful of your digital footprint, and your brand will shine brightly in the online world.

You can shape a positive and influential personal brand that opens doors to opportunities and meaningful connections.

Chapter 5

Content Creation and Sharing

Creating Valuable Content

In the digital era, content is the currency of the internet. Your ability to create valuable, engaging, and relevant content can significantly impact your brand. In this chapter, we will explore the art of content creation, helping you craft compelling messages that resonate with your audience, showcase your expertise, and establish your authority in your field.

1. Understand Your Audience: The key to creating valuable content is knowing your audience inside out. What are their challenges, aspirations, and interests? Tailor your content to address their needs and provide solutions to their problems.

2. Educate and Inform: Position yourself as an expert by creating content that educates and informs your audience. Share insights, industry trends, and expert opinions. Providing valuable information establishes your credibility and builds trust with your audience.

3. Be Authentic: Authenticity is magnetic. Share your personal experiences, successes, and failures. Authentic stories create a genuine connection with your audience, making your content relatable and inspiring.

4. Variety is the Spice of Content: Diversify your content types. Experiment with blog posts, videos, podcasts, infographics, webinars, and social media updates. Different formats cater to different audience preferences, ensuring your message reaches a broader audience.

5. Quality Over Quantity: Focus on quality rather than quantity. A well-researched, well-written, or well-produced piece of content has a far greater impact than multiple mediocre ones. Invest time in creating content that resonates deeply with your audience.

6. Engage and Interact: Encourage engagement by asking questions, conducting polls, or inviting opinions. Respond promptly to comments and messages. Engaging with your audience creates a sense of community and fosters loyalty.

7. SEO Optimization: Understand basic SEO principles to optimize your content for search engines. Use relevant keywords, create compelling headlines, and structure your content for readability. SEO-friendly content ensures your material is discoverable by a wider audience.

8. Consistency is Key: Establish a consistent posting schedule. Whether it's daily, weekly, or monthly, consistency keeps your audience engaged and eagerly anticipating your content. Regularity builds anticipation and strengthens your brand presence.

9. Stay Updated: Stay abreast of industry trends, news, and developments. Share your insights and opinions on relevant topics. Being up-to-date positions you as a thought leader, enhancing your credibility and influence.

10. Measure and Adapt: Use analytics to measure the performance of your content. Identify which pieces resonate most with your audience and adapt your content strategy accordingly. Analytics provide valuable insights into audience preferences and behavior.

Remember, valuable content not only showcases your expertise but also adds genuine value to your audience's lives. By creating content that educates, informs, and inspires, you position yourself as a go-to resource, cultivating a loyal following and establishing your brand as a beacon of knowledge and authenticity. So, go ahead, unleash your creativity, and craft content that leaves a lasting impact.

Content Marketing Strategies

Content marketing is a strategic approach that focuses on creating and distributing valuable, relevant, and consistent content to attract and engage a clearly defined audience. Here are some effective content marketing strategies to elevate your brand:

1. Define Your Goals: Determine your content marketing objectives. Whether it's increasing brand awareness, driving website traffic, generating leads, or establishing expertise, clearly defined goals will shape your content strategy.

2. Know Your Audience: Understand your target audience's needs, preferences, and pain points. Create content that addresses their challenges and provides solutions. Tailoring your content to your audience ensures it resonates and adds value.

3. Content Calendar: Develop a content calendar outlining what, when, and where you'll publish your content. Consistency is key, so plan your content schedule. A calendar helps you stay organized and maintain a regular posting cadence.

4. Multichannel Approach: Utilize various platforms and formats. From blogs and social media to podcasts, videos, and ebooks, diverse content formats cater to different audience preferences and broaden your reach.

5. SEO Optimization: Optimize your content for search engines. Research relevant keywords, incorporate them naturally into your content, and optimize meta tags. SEO-friendly content improves your visibility and search engine rankings.

6. Promotion and Distribution: Don't just create content; actively promote it. Share your content on social media, engage in online communities, collaborate with influencers, and leverage email marketing. Effective promotion ensures your content reaches a wider audience.

7. Content Repurposing: Repurpose your content into different formats. For instance, transform a blog post into a podcast episode, video, or infographic. Repurposing maximizes the value of your content and caters to diverse audience preferences.

Building Thought Leadership

Becoming a thought leader in your field establishes you as an authority, enhancing your personal brand's credibility and influence. Here's how to build and showcase your thought leadership:

1. In-Depth Knowledge: Continuously expand your expertise. Stay informed about industry trends, research, and developments. Deep knowledge forms the foundation of your thought leadership.

2. Thought-Provoking Content: Create content that challenges existing norms, presents unique perspectives and sparks meaningful discussions. Thought-provoking content stimulates critical thinking and positions you as a forward-thinking expert.

3. Networking and Collaboration: Engage with other thought leaders and influencers in your field. Attend conferences, participate in webinars, and collaborate on projects. Networking enhances your visibility and credibility.

4. Publish Authoritative Content: Write whitepapers, research reports, or ebooks on topics relevant to your industry. Authoritative content showcases your expertise and contributes valuable insights to your field.

5. Speaking Engagements: Speak at conferences, workshops, or webinars. Public speaking establishes you as a knowledgeable authority, allowing you to share your expertise directly with a live audience.

6. Media Presence: Contribute articles to reputable publications or be a guest on podcasts and TV shows. Media appearances increase your visibility and position you as an expert source.

7. Educational Initiatives: Offer webinars, workshops, or online courses. Sharing your knowledge directly with others establishes your expertise and fosters a community around your ideas.

By implementing these content marketing strategies and building thought leadership, you position yourself as a respected expert in your field. Thought leadership not only enhances your brand but also contributes valuable insights to your industry, leaving a lasting impact on your audience and peers. Stay consistent, authentic, and innovative, and watch your influence as a thought leader grow.

Stay consistent, authentic, and innovative, and watch your influence as a thought leader grow.

Chapter 6

Networking and Building Relationships

The Art of Networking

Networking is the cornerstone of personal and professional growth. It's not just about exchanging business cards; it's about building genuine connections, nurturing relationships, and fostering mutually beneficial partnerships. In this chapter, we'll explore the art of networking, guiding you through the process of building meaningful connections that can transform your brand and open doors to new opportunities.

1. Be Genuine: Authenticity is key in networking. Be yourself, express genuine interest in others, and approach conversations with sincerity. Authentic connections are more likely to lead to lasting relationships.

2. Active Listening: Practice active listening when engaging with others. Show genuine interest in their stories, experiences, and opinions. Listening attentively not only demonstrates respect but also helps you understand their needs and interests better.

3. Value-Based Networking: Focus on creating value for others. Offer assistance, share valuable insights, and be generous with your knowledge. A giving attitude builds trust and strengthens your reputation in your network.

4. Quality Over Quantity: It's not about the number of connections you have but the quality of those connections. Cultivate a few meaningful relationships rather than trying to collect a vast number of contacts. Quality relationships are more likely to result in meaningful collaborations and opportunities.

5. Follow Up: After networking events or meetings, follow up with your new connections. Send personalized emails expressing your pleasure in meeting them and reiterate your interest in the topics you discussed. Timely follow-ups demonstrate professionalism and genuine interest.

6. Reciprocity: Networking is a two-way street. Be willing to offer help and support to your connections without expecting immediate returns. When you give selflessly, it often comes back to you in unexpected ways.

7. Online Networking: Leverage online platforms like LinkedIn, Twitter, and professional forums to expand your network. Engage in industry-related discussions, share valuable content, and connect with professionals in your field. Online networking broadens your reach and allows you to connect with like-minded individuals globally.

8. Diversify Your Network: Don't limit your network to people in your immediate field or industry. Connect with individuals from diverse backgrounds, professions, and cultures. A diverse network exposes you to different perspectives and widens your horizons.

9. Attend Networking Events: Actively participate in conferences, seminars, workshops, and industry events. These events provide excellent opportunities to meet professionals in your field, engage in discussions, and establish connections. Prepare a brief introduction and practice your elevator pitch for effective networking.

10. Be Respectful of Others' Time: When networking, respect the time and boundaries of your contacts. Be mindful of their schedules and availability. When requesting a meeting or favor, be clear, concise, and respectful of their time commitments.

Remember, networking is not just about what others can do for you; it's also about what you can offer to them. Building strong relationships is an ongoing process that requires patience, effort, and genuine interest in others. By mastering the art of networking, you can create a valuable and supportive network that enhances your brand and opens doors to endless possibilities.

Building Authentic Relationships

Authentic relationships are the bedrock of a strong personal brand. Here's how you can build genuine connections that go beyond surface interactions:

1. Be Vulnerable: Authenticity breeds authenticity. Don't be afraid to show vulnerability and share your true self with others. People appreciate genuine emotions and openness, which deepens the connection.

2. Show Empathy: Empathy is the ability to understand and share the feelings of another. Put yourself in others' shoes, listen actively, and respond empathetically. Showing genuine concern for others' well-being strengthens the emotional bond in relationships.

3. Be Reliable: Consistently follow through on your commitments. Whether it's a promise to help, meet, or collaborate, reliability builds trust. Being dependable reinforces your credibility and strengthens the foundation of your relationships.

4. Celebrate Others' Success: Be genuinely happy for others' achievements and milestones. Celebrating their successes without jealousy or competition demonstrates your support and strengthens the positive energy in your relationship.

5. Respect Differences: Embrace diversity and respect differences of opinion, culture, and background. A respectful attitude fosters a harmonious atmosphere, encouraging open dialogue and understanding between individuals.

6. Be Present: When interacting with others, be fully present. Put away distractions, actively listen, and engage in meaningful conversations. Being present in the moment shows your respect and value for the relationship.

7. Offer Support: Be supportive in both good times and bad. Offer assistance, encouragement, and a listening ear when needed. Being there for others in times of need strengthens the bond and creates a sense of loyalty.

8. Apologize and Forgive: In any relationship, misunderstandings and conflicts may arise. Be willing to apologize when you are wrong, and practice forgiveness when others make mistakes. Letting go of grudges paves the way for healing and stronger relationships.

Leveraging Your Network for Success

1. Clarify Your Needs: Identify your goals and what you need from your network. Whether it's mentorship, business partnerships, or job opportunities, clarifying your needs helps you communicate effectively with your network.

2. Offer Value First: Before seeking assistance, offer value to your network. Provide assistance, share knowledge, or connect people who could benefit from each other. Giving first builds goodwill and increases the likelihood of receiving support when you need it.

3. Be Specific: When seeking help or advice, be specific about what you need. Clear communication helps your network understand how they can assist you effectively. Specific requests receive more focused and helpful responses.

4. Follow Up: After receiving support or advice, follow up with your network to express gratitude and provide updates on your progress. A simple thank-you message shows your appreciation and keeps the relationship positive.

5. Stay Engaged: Regularly engage with your network even when you don't need immediate assistance. Stay updated on their achievements, offer congratulations, and show genuine interest in their well-being. Continuous engagement strengthens relationships over time.

6. Be Genuine: Authenticity is equally important when leveraging your network. Be sincere, honest, and appreciative. People can sense genuine intentions, and authenticity builds trust, making your network more willing to support you.

Building authentic relationships and leveraging your network for success is a reciprocal process. By nurturing genuine connections and approaching your network with sincerity and respect, you create a supportive ecosystem that not only benefits your personal brand but also enriches the lives of everyone involved. Remember, networking is not just a transactional activity; it's about building enduring relationships based on trust, respect, and mutual support.

Chapter 7

Building Authority in Your Field

Becoming an Expert

Chapter 7: Building Authority in Your Field

Authority in your field is the pinnacle of personal branding. When you're seen as an expert, your brand gains credibility, influence, and trust. In this chapter, we will explore how to build authority and establish yourself as an expert in your chosen domain.

Becoming an Expert:

1. **Continuous Learning:** The journey to expertise begins with a commitment to continuous learning. Stay updated with the latest developments, trends, and knowledge in your field. Invest in courses, attend workshops, and read industry-specific literature.

2. **Research and Mastery:** Deepen your knowledge in a specific niche within your field. Specialization often leads to expertise. Conduct research, contribute to the

body of knowledge, and master your chosen area of focus.

3. **Practical Application:** Apply your knowledge and skills to solve real-world problems. Practical experience solidifies your expertise and provides tangible examples of your competence.

4. **Mentorship and Collaboration:** Seek guidance from mentors and collaborate with industry experts. Learning from those who have already achieved authority can fast-track your path to expertise.

5. **Share Your Knowledge:** Don't hoard your knowledge; share it generously. Write articles, give presentations, and contribute to discussions in your field. Sharing your insights and expertise demonstrates your commitment to your field.

6. **Publish Authoritative Content:** Write whitepapers, research papers, or books related to your field. Authoritative content showcases your expertise and contributes valuable insights to your industry.

7. **Speak at Conferences:** Present your research or insights at conferences, seminars, and workshops. Public speaking not only positions you as a knowledgeable

authority but also offers the opportunity to network with peers.

8. **Teaching and Training:** Offer workshops or training sessions to transfer your knowledge to others. Teaching not only reinforces your understanding but also establishes you as an expert in your field.

9. **Media Presence:** Contribute articles to well-regarded publications and be a guest on podcasts or television shows. Media appearances increase your visibility and help you reach a wider audience.

10. **Awards and Recognitions:** Seek industry awards and recognitions. Nominations and accolades from your peers and industry organizations solidify your authority.

11. **Networking with Influencers:** Engage with influencers and thought leaders in your field. Collaborations and endorsements from recognized experts can enhance your authority.

12. **Build a Portfolio:** Create a portfolio of work, research, or projects that showcase your expertise. A strong portfolio provides tangible proof of your capabilities.

Becoming an expert is a gradual process that requires dedication, perseverance, and a genuine passion for your field. It's not just about what you know; it's about how you apply and share your knowledge. By continually improving your skills, sharing your insights, and seeking opportunities to contribute to your field, you can ascend to the ranks of authority in your chosen domain. Building authority not only enhances your brand but also makes a meaningful impact in your industry.

Sharing Your Expertise

Sharing your expertise is not only a way to give back to your community but also a powerful method to strengthen your brand. Here's how you can effectively share your knowledge and skills with others:

1. Blogging: Start a blog in your niche. Write insightful articles, how-to guides, and opinion pieces related to your field. Regularly updating your blog with valuable content establishes you as a reliable source of information.

2. Social Media: Utilize social media platforms to share bite-sized knowledge. Post tips, infographics, and short videos. Engage with your followers by answering questions and participating in discussions related to your expertise.

3. Online Courses and Webinars: Create online courses or host webinars on platforms like Udemy, Coursera, or Zoom. Sharing in-depth knowledge demonstrates your expertise and provides valuable learning experiences for your audience.

4. Podcasting: Start a podcast where you discuss industry trends, interview experts, and share insights. Podcasts are an excellent medium for reaching a broader audience and establishing your authority through thoughtful discussions.

5. Guest Blogging and Interviews: Contribute guest posts to reputable websites and blogs within your industry. Participate in interviews on podcasts, YouTube channels, or blogs. Being featured as an expert enhances your credibility and exposes you to new audiences.

6. YouTube Channel: Create educational videos on YouTube. Visual content is engaging and allows you to demonstrate your expertise effectively. Tutorials, product reviews, and industry insights can attract a dedicated subscriber base.

7. Networking Events: Speak at conferences, seminars, and workshops. Sharing your expertise in front of a live audience enhances your credibility and positions you as an expert in your field.

Establishing Credibility

1. Consistency: Consistency in delivering accurate and valuable information is essential. Ensure your messages are coherent across all platforms. Inconsistencies can damage your credibility.

2. Research and Data: Support your statements with credible research and data. Facts and figures from reputable sources add weight to your expertise and establish you as a knowledgeable authority.

3. Testimonials and Case Studies: Collect testimonials from satisfied clients, colleagues, or students. Share success stories and case studies that highlight the positive impact of your expertise. Real-life examples provide tangible evidence of your capabilities.

4. Professional Certifications: Obtain relevant certifications and credentials in your field. Certifications from reputable institutions enhance your credibility and demonstrate your commitment to continuous learning.

5. Peer Recognition: Receive endorsements and recommendations from peers and industry experts. Peer recognition reinforces your credibility within your professional community.

6. Transparency: Be transparent about your expertise and experience. Honesty about your strengths and limitations fosters trust. If you don't know the answer to a question, admit it, and commit to finding accurate information.

7. Quality Content: Ensure the quality of your content. Well-researched, well-written, and well-presented content reflects professionalism and adds to your credibility.

Remember, credibility is built over time through a consistent demonstration of expertise, reliability, and trustworthiness. By sharing your knowledge generously and establishing your credibility through various means, you not only enhance your brand but also contribute positively to your field, earning the respect and trust of your peers and audience.

Chapter 8

Measuring and Monitoring Your Brand's Success

Key Performance Indicators (KPIs)

Understanding the impact of your brand is crucial for its continuous growth and refinement. In this chapter, we'll delve into the importance of measuring and monitoring your brand's success, along with the essential Key Performance Indicators (KPIs) that can provide valuable insights into your brand's performance.

Why Measure Your Brand's Success:

1. Identify Progress: Monitoring your brand's performance allows you to track your progress over time. By analyzing data, you can identify trends, successes, and areas that need improvement.

2. Strategic Decision Making: Data-driven insights enable you to make informed decisions about your brand strategy. Understanding what works and what doesn't empowers you to refine your approach and focus your efforts effectively.

3. Enhance ROI: Measuring the success of your brand helps you assess the return on investment (ROI) of your time, energy, and resources. You can optimize your efforts based on what yields the best results.

Key Performance Indicators (KPIs) for Personal Branding

1. Online Presence Metrics:
Website Traffic: Measure the number of visitors to your website. Track unique visitors, page views, and bounce rates to understand user engagement.

Social Media Engagement: Monitor likes, shares, comments, and follower growth across your social media platforms.

Search Engine Ranking: Track your website's ranking on search engine results pages (SERPs) for relevant keywords. Higher rankings indicate better visibility.

2. Content Engagement:
Blog Views: Measure the number of views, likes, and shares on your blog posts. Analyze which topics resonate most with your audience.

Video Views: Track the views, likes, and comments on your videos. Video engagement metrics provide insights into your audience's preferences.

3. Audience Growth and Demographics:
Follower Growth: Monitor the growth rate of your social media followers. Analyze which platforms attract the most followers and engagement.

Demographic Insights: Understand your audience's demographics, including age, location, gender, and interests. Tailor your content based on this information.

4. Engagement Metrics:

Email Open Rates: Measure the percentage of recipients who open your emails. Higher open rates indicate compelling subject lines and relevant content.

Conversion Rates: Track the conversion rates for specific actions, such as signing up for newsletters or downloading resources. Conversion data reflects the effectiveness of your calls to action.

5. Influence and Authority:

Media Mentions: Count the number of times you are mentioned in media outlets, blogs, or industry publications.

Speaking Engagements: Measure the number of invitations to speak at conferences, webinars, or podcasts. Speaking engagements signify your recognition as an industry expert.

6. Client or Audience Feedback:

Surveys and Feedback Forms: Collect feedback from clients, readers, or event attendees through surveys. Analyze qualitative data to understand their satisfaction levels and preferences.

7. *Brand Sentiment Analysis:*

Social Media Sentiment: Use sentiment analysis tools to gauge the sentiment (positive, negative, or neutral) of mentions related to your brand on social media platforms.

8. *Network Growth and Engagement:*

Professional Network Growth: Track the growth of your professional network on platforms like LinkedIn. Analyze the level of engagement within your network, including endorsements and recommendations.

Regularly monitoring these KPIs provides a comprehensive view of your personal brand's performance. It allows you to adjust your strategies, capitalize on successful tactics, and address areas that require improvement. Remember, personal branding is an ongoing process, and analyzing these metrics helps you refine your brand for maximum impact and relevance in your field.

Tracking and Analyzing Your Progress

Tracking and analyzing your progress is essential to understanding the effectiveness of your personal branding efforts. Here's how you can effectively monitor your progress and make data-driven decisions:

1. Set Clear Goals: Establish specific, measurable, attainable, relevant, and time-bound (SMART) goals for your brand. Clearly defined objectives provide a basis for measurement and evaluation.

2. Use Analytics Tools: Utilize various analytics tools and platforms to track your website traffic, social media engagement, email open rates, and other relevant metrics. Google Analytics, social media insights, and email marketing software provide detailed data on user behavior and interactions.

3. Regularly Review Key Metrics: Monitor key performance indicators (KPIs) regularly. Set specific intervals (weekly, monthly, quarterly) to review your metrics. Identify trends, patterns, and areas of improvement.

4. Analyze Audience Feedback: Pay attention to feedback from your audience. Surveys, comments, and direct messages can provide valuable insights into audience preferences and satisfaction levels.

5. Compare Against Goals: Compare your actual performance against the goals you set. Assess whether you're meeting, exceeding, or falling short of your objectives. Analyze the reasons behind the outcomes.

6. Identify Successful Strategies: Determine which branding strategies and activities yield the best results. Identify the types of content, platforms, or communication styles that resonate most with your audience.

7. **Track Audience Growth:** Monitor the growth of your online and offline audience. Assess follower/subscriber growth rates, and identify periods of significant growth or decline.

Adjusting Your Branding Strategy

1. Iterative Improvement: Personal branding is an iterative process. Use the insights gathered from tracking and analysis to refine your strategies continuously. Experiment with new approaches based on what you've learned.

2. Focus on Strengths: Identify your strengths and areas where you excel. Focus your branding strategy on highlighting these strengths. Authenticity and genuine passion are powerful brand attributes.

3. Address Weaknesses: Acknowledge areas where you may be lacking or facing challenges. Develop strategies to improve in these areas, whether it's enhancing specific skills or addressing negative feedback.

4. Adapt to Audience Feedback: Listen to your audience. If certain content or messages resonate better, tailor your strategy to align with your audience's preferences. Be adaptable and responsive to their needs.

5. Stay Current: Stay updated with industry trends and changes in your field. Your branding strategy should evolve to align with the latest developments. Continuous learning keeps your brand relevant and forward-thinking.

6. Collaborate and Network: Collaborate with others in your field. Networking and partnerships can introduce you to new audiences and provide fresh perspectives. Collaborative projects enhance your credibility and reach.

7. Seek Professional Guidance: If necessary, seek the assistance of professionals such as marketing experts, personal branding consultants, or career coaches. Their expertise can provide valuable insights and strategies tailored to your specific goals.

8. Celebrate Milestones: Acknowledge and celebrate your achievements and milestones. Recognizing your progress boosts morale and motivation, fueling your drive to continue improving your brand.

Remember, personal branding is a dynamic and evolving process. By tracking your progress, analyzing data, and adjusting your strategies based on insights and feedback, you can create a personal brand that truly resonates with your audience and sets you apart in your field. Stay agile, receptive, and committed to continuous improvement, and your brand will thrive.

You can create a personal brand that truly resonates with your audience and sets you apart in your field.

Chapter 9

Overcoming Common Personal Branding Challenges

Dealing with Impostor Syndrome

Building a personal brand is a rewarding journey, but it comes with its own set of challenges. In this chapter, we will address one of the most prevalent hurdles faced by individuals striving to establish their personal brand: Impostor Syndrome, and how to overcome it.

Impostor Syndrome is a psychological pattern where an individual doubts their accomplishments and has a persistent fear of being exposed as a "fraud," despite evident success or external validation. Here's how you can overcome Impostor Syndrome in the context of personal branding:

1. Acknowledge Your Feelings: Accept that feeling like a fraud is a common experience, especially when stepping into the spotlight. Many successful individuals have battled Impostor Syndrome. Acknowledging your feelings is the first step toward overcoming them.

2. Separate Feelings from Facts: Recognize that your feelings of inadequacy are not facts. Challenge negative self-talk and irrational beliefs. List your accomplishments, skills, and experiences to remind yourself of your capabilities.

3. Normalize Mistakes: Understand that making mistakes is a natural part of the learning process. Instead of viewing failures as proof of your incompetence, see them as opportunities to learn and grow. Embrace the lessons they offer.

4. Set Realistic Expectations: Avoid setting unrealistic standards for yourself. It's okay to have high aspirations, but understand that everyone, even the most successful individuals, faces setbacks and challenges. Perfection is not a realistic or attainable goal.

5. Seek Support: Talk to trusted friends, mentors, or a therapist about your feelings. Sharing your concerns with others who understand can provide valuable perspective and reassurance. Often, you'll find that you are not alone in experiencing these feelings.

6. Focus on Progress, Not Perfection: Instead of aiming for flawless execution, focus on progress and growth. Celebrate your achievements, no matter how small they may seem. Every step forward is a testament to your abilities.

7. Practice Self-Compassion: Treat yourself with the same kindness and understanding that you would offer to a friend. Be compassionate with yourself when you make mistakes or face challenges. Self-compassion fosters resilience and self-confidence.

8. Visualize Success: Create a mental image of your success. Visualization techniques can help boost your confidence and diminish feelings of inadequacy. Imagine yourself confidently navigating challenging situations and achieving your goals.

9. Embrace Learning: Embrace the mindset of a lifelong learner. View challenges as opportunities to acquire new skills and knowledge. The process of learning and growing can boost your confidence and dispel feelings of impostorism.

10. Celebrate Your Unique Qualities: Embrace what makes you unique. Your individuality and diverse experiences contribute to your personal brand. Celebrate your authenticity and use it as a source of strength.

Remember, overcoming Impostor Syndrome is a gradual process that requires patience and self-compassion. By challenging negative self-perceptions, seeking support, and reframing your mindset, you can build a resilient personal brand that reflects your true capabilities and accomplishments. Don't let Impostor Syndrome hold you back; instead, let it become a stepping stone toward greater self-awareness and confidence in your personal branding journey.

Handling Criticism and Negative Feedback

Receiving criticism and negative feedback is an inevitable part of building a personal brand. Here's how you can handle criticism constructively and use it as a tool for growth:

1. Remain Calm: When faced with criticism, take a deep breath and remain calm. Avoid reacting impulsively. Emotions can cloud your judgment; a composed response demonstrates maturity and professionalism.

2. Seek Constructive Feedback: Differentiate between constructive criticism and baseless negativity. Constructive feedback offers specific suggestions for improvement. Embrace it as an opportunity to learn and enhance your skills.

3. Reflect and Evaluate: Reflect on the criticism objectively. Evaluate whether there is merit in the feedback. Consider if the criticism aligns with your goals and values. Honest self-reflection helps you glean valuable insights.

4. Respond Professionally: If a response is necessary, craft a professional and polite reply. Acknowledge the feedback, express gratitude for the input, and share your perspective respectfully. A diplomatic response shows maturity.

5. Learn and Improve: Use criticism as a catalyst for improvement. Analyze the feedback and identify areas where you can grow. Continuous self-improvement strengthens your brand in the long run.

6. Develop Resilience: Develop resilience to negative feedback. Understand that not everyone will appreciate your work or personal brand. Focus on your supporters and positive interactions rather than dwelling on negativity.

Staying Authentic

Authenticity is the cornerstone of a strong personal brand. Here's how you can stay true to yourself while building your brand:

1. Know Your Values: Define your core values and principles. Your brand should align with these values. Knowing what you stand for helps you make authentic choices in your personal and professional life.

2. Be Transparent: Be open about your experiences, both successes and failures. Sharing your journey authentically makes you relatable and fosters genuine connections with your audience.

3. Honest Communication: Practice honest and transparent communication. Speak your truth respectfully and genuinely. Avoid exaggeration or misrepresentation; authenticity shines through sincerity.

4. Embrace Vulnerability: Don't be afraid to show vulnerability. Authenticity comes from embracing your imperfections and sharing your genuine self. Vulnerability fosters deep connections and relatability.

5. Stay Consistent: Be consistent in your actions, values, and messaging. Consistency builds trust. Your audience should recognize your authenticity in every aspect of your brand.

6. Avoid Comparisons: Resist the urge to compare yourself to others. Authenticity thrives when you focus on your unique qualities and experiences. Embrace your individuality; it sets you apart.

7. Trust Your Instincts: Listen to your intuition. Trust your instincts when making decisions related to your brand. Your authentic self often guides you in the right direction.

8. Celebrate Your Uniqueness: Embrace what makes you unique. Your quirks, experiences, and perspectives contribute to your authenticity. Celebrate your individuality; it's what makes your brand stand out.

Building a personal brand requires resilience, self-awareness, and a commitment to authenticity. By handling criticism gracefully and staying true to your values and identity, you not only strengthen your brand but also inspire trust and loyalty among your audience. Authenticity is a magnet that attracts genuine connections and opportunities, making your brand a true reflection of your unique and authentic self.

Chapter 10

Taking Your Career to the Next Level

Leveraging Your Brand for Career Advancement

Congratulations! You've built a strong personal brand, but your journey doesn't end here. In this final chapter, we'll explore how to leverage your well-crafted personal brand to propel your career to new heights.

1. Networking and Partnerships: Utilize your brand to expand your professional network. Connect with influencers, industry leaders, and like-minded professionals. Collaborate on projects, attend conferences, and engage in networking events. These connections can open doors to new opportunities and collaborations.

2. Job Opportunities: Your brand can attract job offers and career opportunities. Recruiters and employers often seek out individuals with a strong online presence and expertise in their field. Stay active on professional platforms like LinkedIn, showcasing your achievements, skills, and projects.

3. Thought Leadership: Continue to establish yourself as a thought leader in your industry. Write articles, give talks, and share your expertise through various channels. As a recognized authority, you become a go-to person for insights, increasing your visibility and credibility.

4. Mentorship and Coaching: Use your brand to offer mentorship or coaching services. Share your experiences and knowledge with others, guiding them in their career journeys. Mentorship not only helps others but also enhances your reputation as a leader in your field.

5. Consulting and Freelancing: Leverage your expertise to offer consulting services or freelance work. Your brand serves as a portfolio showcasing your skills and achievements. Clients are more likely to trust and hire individuals with a strong personal brand.

6. Public Speaking Engagements: Secure speaking opportunities at conferences, webinars, and workshops. Public speaking enhances your visibility and positions you as an expert. Use these platforms to share your insights, connect with your audience, and expand your influence.

7. Collaborative Projects: Collaborate with other professionals on joint projects. Whether it's writing a book, launching a podcast, or organizing an event, collaborative ventures broaden your reach and introduce you to new audiences.

8. Continuous Learning: Stay updated with industry trends and new skills. Continuously investing in your education and skill set ensures you remain relevant and competitive. Attend workshops, take online courses, and obtain certifications to enhance your expertise.

9. Public Relations and Media Appearances: Work with public relations professionals to secure media appearances. Being featured in newspapers, magazines, podcasts, and TV shows enhances your visibility and credibility. Media exposure can significantly elevate your career.

10. Feedback and Adaptation: Continuously seek feedback from your audience and peers. Be open to constructive criticism and adapt your approach based on insights. A willingness to evolve and improve strengthens your brand over time.

Remember, your brand is not static; it's a living entity that evolves with your experiences and achievements. By leveraging your brand effectively, you can not only advance your career but also make a meaningful impact in your industry. Stay authentic, stay passionate, and continue to build upon the foundation you've established. Your brand has the power to shape your future and pave the way for endless possibilities in your professional journey.

Entrepreneurship and Personal Branding

Entrepreneurship and personal branding are intertwined in the modern business landscape. As an entrepreneur, your brand is not just your identity; it's a powerful tool that can drive the success of your business. Here's how to leverage personal branding in the entrepreneurial journey:

1. Authentic Storytelling: Share your entrepreneurial journey authentically. People connect with stories, especially those of struggle, perseverance, and triumph. Your personal brand story can inspire others and create emotional connections with your audience.

2. Building Trust: Trust is vital in business. A strong personal brand exuding authenticity, expertise, and integrity builds trust with customers, investors, and partners. Trust in your brand translates into trust in your business.

3. Expert Positioning: Position yourself as an expert in your industry. Share your knowledge, insights, and experiences through blogs, videos, podcasts, and social media. Establish yourself as a thought leader to attract a loyal following and gain credibility.

4. Networking and Partnerships: Leverage your brand to network with potential collaborators, investors, and mentors. A well-established personal brand opens doors to strategic partnerships, funding opportunities, and valuable mentorship.

5. Customer Relationships: Engage with your customers on a personal level. Respond to their queries, address their concerns, and show appreciation for their support. Personalized interactions strengthen customer loyalty and enhance your brand reputation.

6. Innovative Marketing: Use your brand creatively in marketing strategies. You can be the face of your business, appearing in advertisements, social media campaigns, and promotional events. Your brand adds a human touch to your marketing efforts.

7. Handling Challenges: Your brand can help you navigate challenges. During tough times, your reputation and the relationships you've built through your brand can rally support, whether it's from customers, investors, or the wider community.

Achieving Your Career Goals

Achieving your career goals requires a combination of strategic planning, continuous learning, and effective personal branding.

1. Set Clear Goals: Define your short-term and long-term career goals. Make them specific, measurable, achievable, relevant, and time-bound (SMART). Clear goals provide direction and motivation.

2. Develop a Personal Branding Strategy: Create a personal branding strategy aligned with your career objectives. Identify your unique value proposition, target audience, and key messages. Your brand should reflect your career goals and aspirations.

3. Continuous Learning: Invest in continuous learning and skill development. Stay updated with industry trends, acquire new skills, and pursue certifications or advanced degrees if they align with your career path.

4. Networking and Mentorship: Build a strong professional network. Connect with peers, mentors, and industry leaders. Networking opens doors to new opportunities, collaborations, and valuable advice. Mentorship provides guidance and insights from experienced professionals.

5. Embrace Challenges: Don't shy away from challenges; view them as opportunities for growth. Overcoming obstacles builds resilience and strengthens your skillset. Embracing challenges demonstrates your ability to adapt and thrive.

6. Track Your Progress: Regularly assess your progress toward your career goals. Reflect on your achievements, challenges faced, and lessons learned. Use this reflection to adjust your strategies and set new milestones.

7. Stay Adaptable: The business landscape evolves rapidly. Stay adaptable and open to change. Be willing to explore new roles, industries, or entrepreneurial ventures if they align with your passions and skills.

8. Work-Life Balance: Maintain a healthy work-life balance. Balance your professional ambitions with personal well-being, family time, and hobbies. A balanced life ensures sustained energy and enthusiasm for your career pursuits.

9. Celebrate Milestones: Celebrate your achievements and milestones, no matter how small. Acknowledging your progress boosts morale and motivation, fueling your drive to achieve greater heights.

Conclusion

In the pages of this book, we embarked on a transformative journey, exploring the art and science of personal branding. We delved into the nuances of crafting an authentic and compelling personal brand, from defining your unique value proposition to leveraging it for career advancement and entrepreneurship. With every chapter, we unearthed the secrets to becoming an authority in your field, achieving your career goals, and navigating the challenges that come your way.

Armed with the knowledge of building a successful personal brand, you are now equipped to embark on a remarkable voyage, a journey not just in the professional realm but also toward self-discovery and empowerment. Your brand is not just a logo, a tagline, or a set of skills; it's the essence of who you are, distilled into a powerful narrative that resonates with the world.

As you step into the world with your refined personal brand, remember that your journey doesn't end here; it evolves. Stay curious, keep learning, and remain adaptable. Embrace challenges as opportunities for growth, and let your authenticity shine brightly in every endeavor.

In the realm of personal branding, your story is your most potent asset, and the world is waiting to hear it. Your unique experiences, skills, and passions are the ingredients that shape your personal brand's narrative. The impact you make, the connections you forge, and the legacy you leave behind, all are reflections of the authentic personal brand you've cultivated.

Go forth with confidence, embrace your uniqueness, and let your brand be a guiding light, illuminating your path toward unparalleled success. The world is ready to witness the incredible story of your journey, beautifully etched through the canvas of your personal brand. So, step into your future with purpose, and let your brand speak volumes, leaving an indelible mark on the world.